Robots 1:2

T0372281

robots were meant to be toys, of course, but we regard them as small kinetic sculptures of surprising originality, and we take pleasure in the thought that anonymous designers – under considerable cost constraints and in quick succession – invented these fantastic lithographed creatures with their peculiar movements, bringing the tin to life.

Robots and astronauts accompanied the post-war fantasy of colonizing space, based on rocket technology developed during the Second World War. The rivalry between the United States and the Soviet Union accelerated the space race and the majority of such toys – destined for the US market – represent the American quest.

What fascinates us about robots is that they are not derived from an existing creature, in contrast to almost every other type of figurative toy (doll/human, teddy bear/bear, Mickey Mouse/mouse), but based on free invention. Their predecessors and role models come from the realms of literature and cinema.

Robots remain disconcerting and enigmatic, springing from a philosophical debate about mechanical servants and the dialectics of master/slave. This aspect was emphasized in the 2001 presentation of our collection by Diller/Scofidio at the Fondation Cartier in Paris.

Constructed for obedience and work, they are machines, but they have humanoid characteristics. They liberate their masters from tedious tasks, yet this creates dependency. Will they someday rebel? In Karel Čapek's science fiction play *R.U.R.* from 1920, the first servant robots appear. They ultimately take revenge on their masters, and in the current discourse on artificial intelligence, there is an expressed fear that the continual self-optimization of AI will eventually lead to its autonomy and the

In 2018 we published the book *Robots 1:1*, which featured photographic illustrations of 148 robotic toys and astronaut figures in their actual size. Issued in a signed edition of 1000 copies, the large-format book was out of print within a few months.

As the title *Robots 1:2* indicates, the robots in this subsequent publication are depicted at half-size. A number of robotic figures from the former Soviet Union and robot-driven space toys have been added, and the book comes at a much lower price.

The robots are shown in chronological order with the corresponding packaging box on the opposite page. As boxes are typically discarded after a short time, they are even rarer than the robots. The illustrations on the boxes offer insights into the space-age fantasies of the era.

The robotic and astronaut figures presented here were manufactured in the period between 1937 and 1976, mainly in Japan. All of the robots have a mechanical device and perform an animated action. By scanning the QR code assigned to a number of robots, readers can observe the figures in motion. The movements and sounds are essential in order to fully appreciate the fascination of these robots.

Visitors to the Vitra Campus in Weil am Rhein, Germany, can view an installation of the Robots and Space Toys collection in the so-called *Wunderkammer*, together with circus objects, comic book characters, merchandising products and folk art (see the Vitra Design Museum website).

Our gratitude goes to Thorsten Romanus for the book design and to Luka Dogan for the short videos of the robots in action.

Rolf Fehlbaum   Fifo Stricker

«It is this lack of self-consciousness on the part of the real toymaker, his complete involvement with the spirit of the toy, that enables him to take the meanest material and make it sing.» [1]

Charles Eames

[1] Eames Demetrios and Carla Hartman, eds, *Essential Eames: Words & Pictures* (Weil am Rhein: Vitra Design Museum, 2017), 156.

Robot Lilliput   6
P: KT
D: Kuramochi Shoten, CK
clockwork
Japan 1937
15.2 cm

P: Producer
D: Distributor

Watch
this object
in motion

Atomic Robot Man
clockwork
Japan 1949
12.7 cm

Space Car
P: Usagiya
D: Linemar
friction
Japan 1950's
7.5 cm

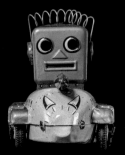
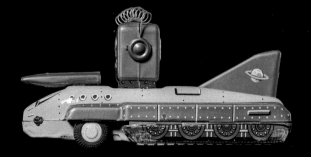

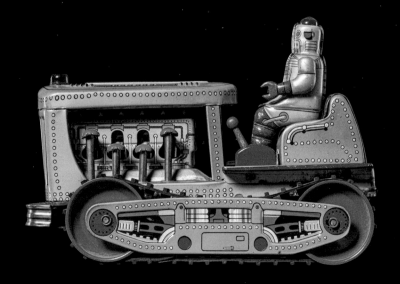

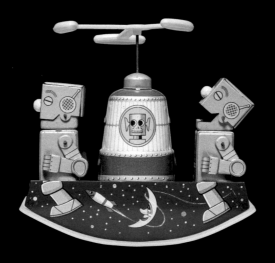

ROBOT TORPEDO

ROBOT TORPEDO

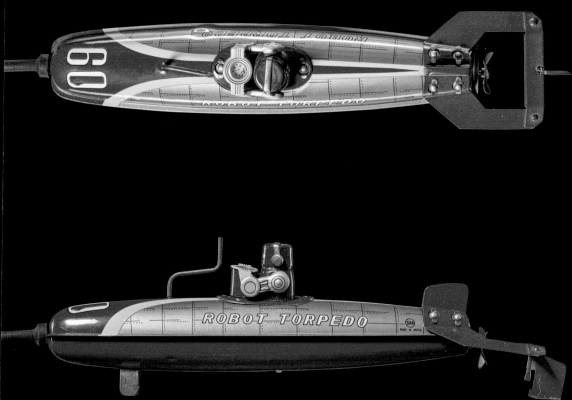

»Marvelous Mike
Electromatic Tractor«
P: Saunders
battery operated
USA 1955
21 cm

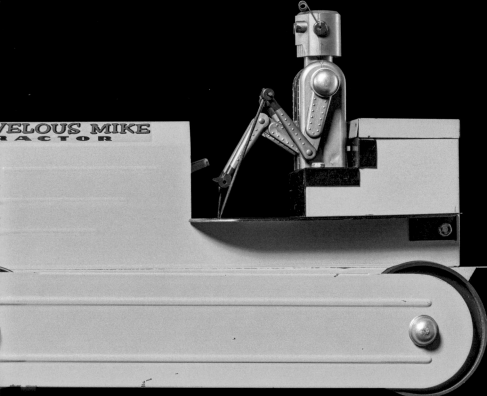

ZOOMER The ROBOT
Battery Operated
TRADE T.N MA
JAPAN
PATENT
SHOWA

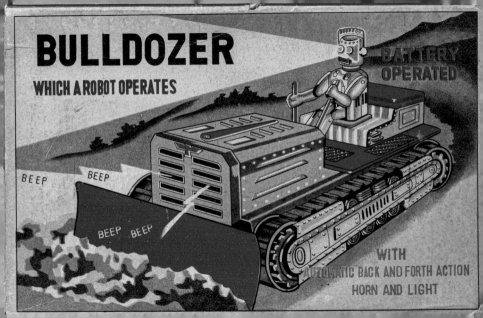

BATTERY OPERATED
ROBOT

JAPAN

ELECTRIC
REMOTE
CONTROL
BATTERY OPERATED

EYES LIGHT UP

ARMS SWING

WALKS FORWARD BACKWARD

ELECTRIC
ROBOT
and Son

ADJUSTABLE
ANTENNA
WILL TURN
RIGHT

THE EYES
LIGHT UP
WILL TURN
LEFT

HAS
BUZZER
FOR
SENDING
MORSE
CODE

ONE OF THE MANY MARX TOYS
Have You All of them?

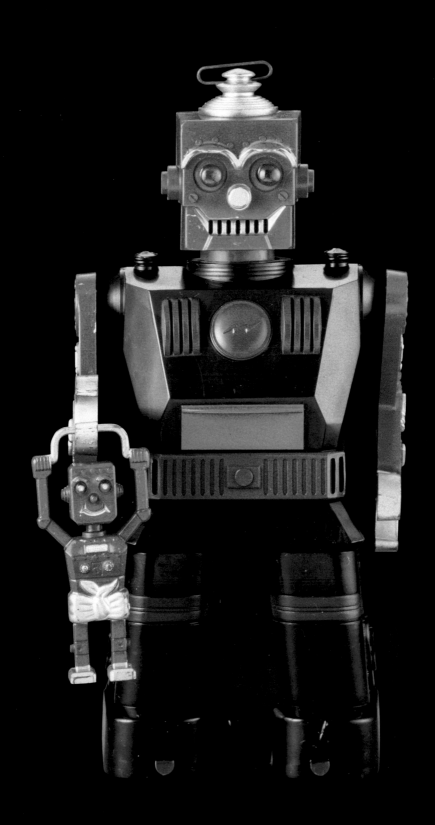

Robot ST 1
P: Strenco
clockwork
West Germany 1955
20 cm

Battery Operated Tractor
P: Nomura
battery operated
Japan 1956
15 cm

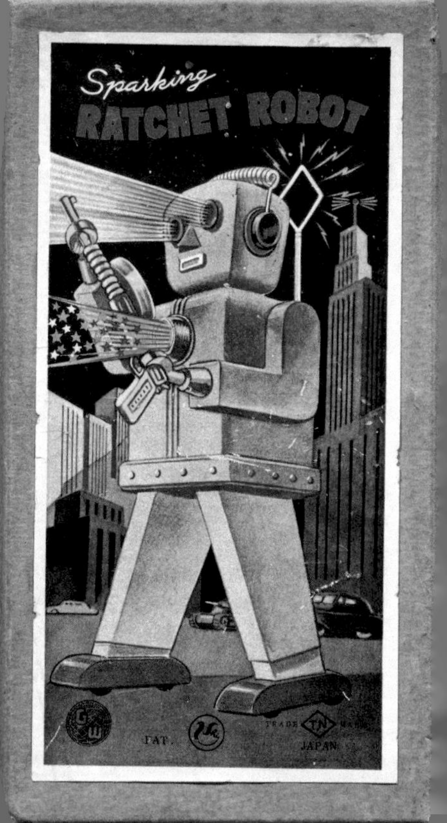
Sparking
RATCHET ROBOT
PAT.
TRADE TN MARK
JAPAN

FRICTION
SPACE
PATROL
ROBBOT ON ROCKET
Zman
Z
TRADE K MARK
MADE IN JAPAN

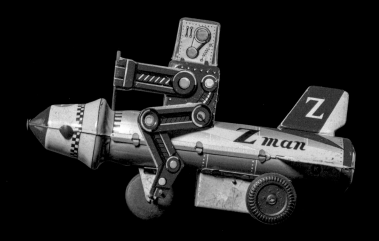

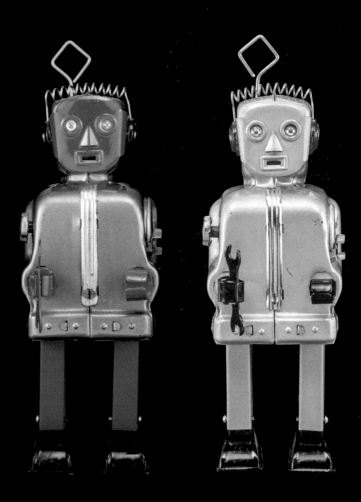

Sparky Robot
P: Yoshiya, KO
clockwork
Japan 1956
19.8 cm

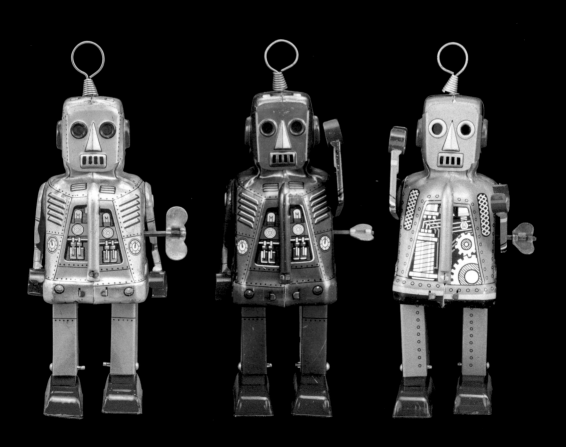

"FLASHY JIM"

THE ROBOT

R7

ACE
JAPAN

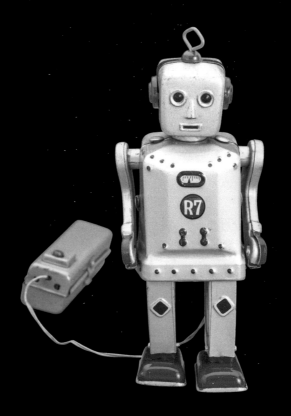

Sparky Robot
P: Yoshiya, KO
clockwork
Japan 1956
19.8 cm

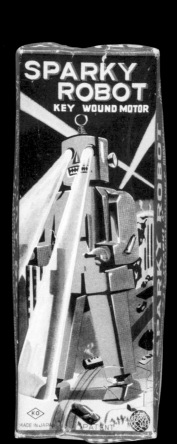

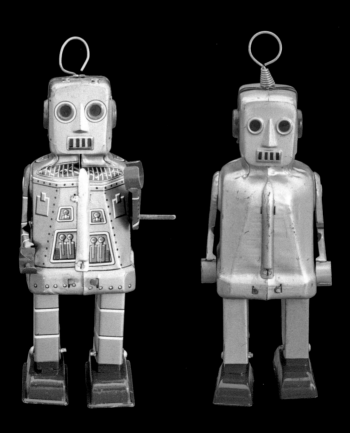

MECHANICAL
ROBOT

IT'S AN I.G.E. TOY

MR. ROBOT

THE MECHANICAL BRAIN

Watch lights go on and off while he walks.
Operates on flashlight batteries.
Make him walk by winding up spring mechahism.

PAT. 30-3023   PAT. 30-11313

TRADE MARK
ALPS
JAPAN

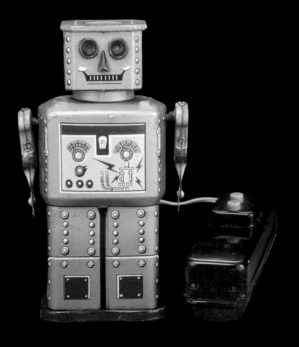

Robbie the Roving Robot
P: SNK
clockwork
Japan 1957
19 cm

Robot
«Easelback Robot»
P: Yonezawa, Y
battery operated
Japan 1957
15 cm

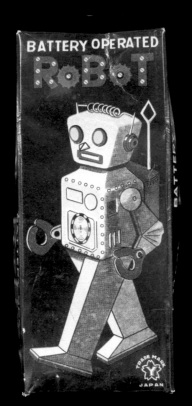

RADAR ROBOT

BLINKING LITE

BRILLIANT LITE
IN EACH EYE

MADE IN JAPAN
TN MARK
PATENT

BATTERY OPERATED
REMOTE CONTROL

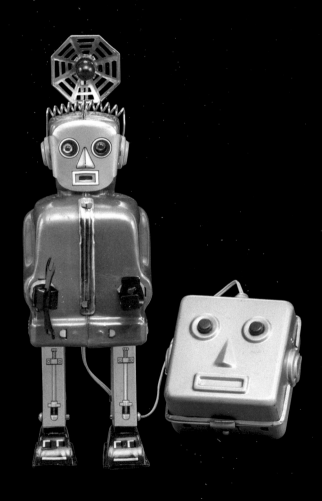

37.2 cm

RADICON ROBOT

RADIO REMOTE
CONTROL ROBOT

THE FIRST AND ONLY
COMPLETE RADIO REMOTE
CONTROL TOY !

RADICON
ROBOT

OFF-ON

PATENTS PENDING: U.S.A.—514190.
CANADA—696947. ENGLAND—92822.
GERMANY—S.46643. DUTCH—93822.
PATENT No. 222956, 237229, 462766
IN JAPAN.

Interplanetary Explorer Spaceman
P: Naito Shoten
clockwork
Japan 1957
20 cm

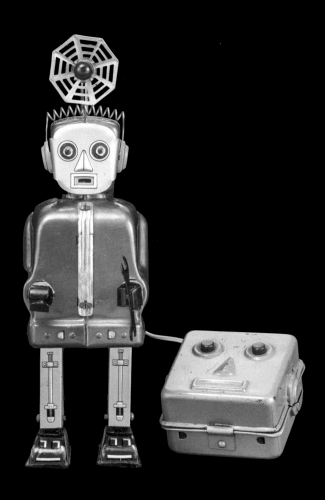

SPACE MAN
BATTERY OPERATED
REMOTE CONTROL
IT'S Cragstan FOR TOYS

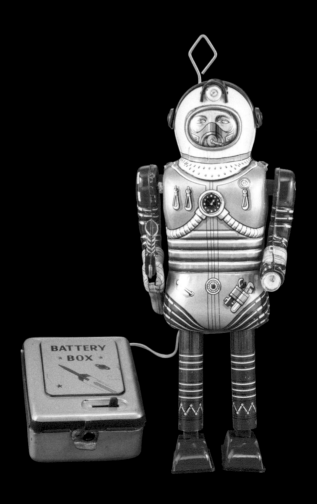

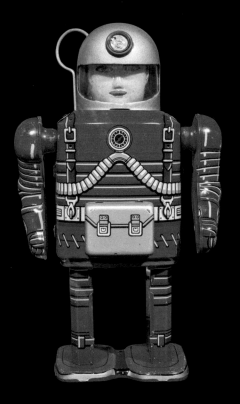

MECHANICAL
DEEP·SEA
ROBOT

AHI
BRAND TOYS

NO. 5823

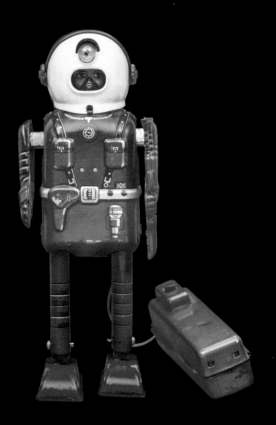

Susie Robette
P: The Metalware Corp.
battery operated
USA 1957
28 cm

MECHANIZED
ROBOT
BATTERY OPERATED
CLEAR PLASTIC DOME LIGHTS UP...SEE THE PISTONS IN ACTION!
ADJUSTABLE ARMS
AMAZING BATTERY OPERATED MECHA NIZED ROBOT
TRADE T.N MARK
MADE IN JAPAN
SHOWA
PAT. PEND.

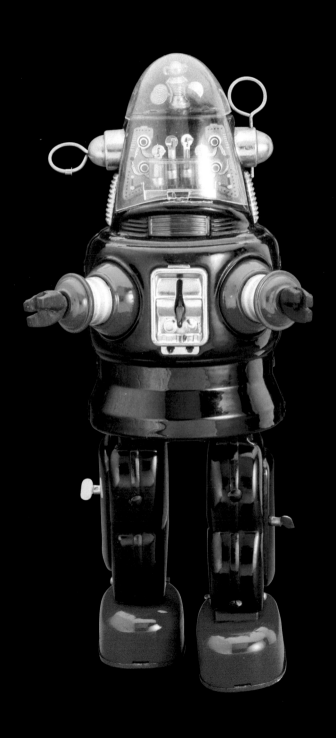

MECHANIZED
ROBOT
BATTERY OPERATED
CLEAR PLASTIC DOME
LIGHTS UP...SEE THE
PISTONS IN ACTION!
ADJUSTABLE
ARMS
AMAZING BATTERY
OPERATED MECHA
NIZED ROBOT
TRADE T.N MARK
MADE IN JAPAN
SHOWA
PAT. PEND.

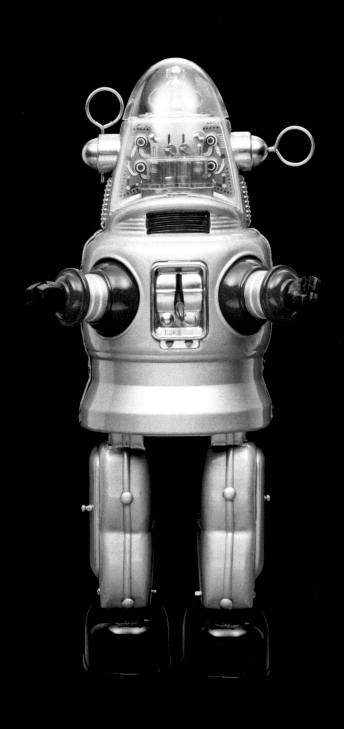

BATTERY OPERATED
ROBOT

WITH AUTOMATIC BACK
AND FORTH ACTION

JAPAN

REMOTE CONTROL
PISTON ACTION
ROBOT
BATTERY OPERATED

PLASTIC DOME
LITES UP!

SEE PISTONS
MOVING UP AND
DOWN IN LITED
PISTON CYLINDERS

ADJUSTABLE
ARMS!!

OPERATES ON
FLASHLITE BATTERIES

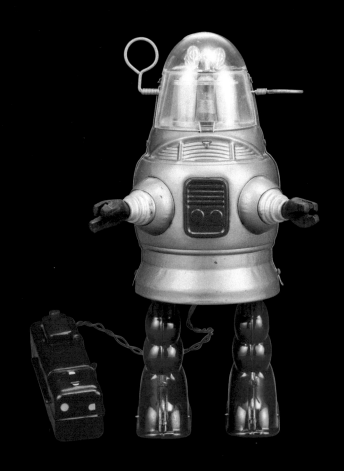

P: Nomura
battery operated
Japan 1957
34 cm

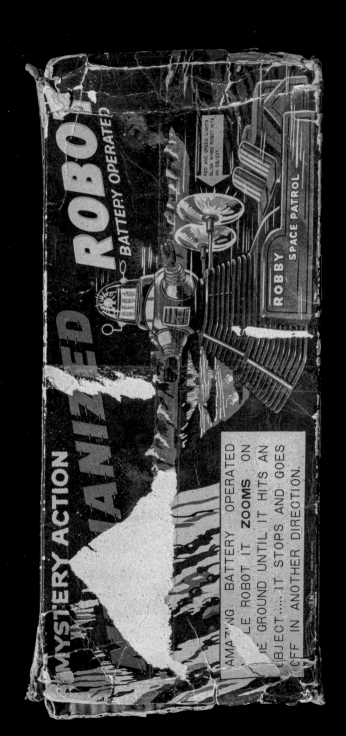

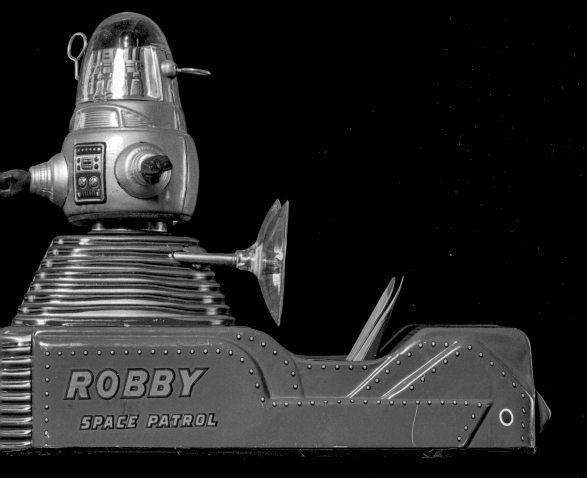

Robotrac »Bulldozer
with Horn and Light«
P: KKS Komoda Shoten
D: Linemar
battery operated
Japan 1957
17 cm

Revolving Flashing Robot
«Door Robot»
P: Alps
battery operated
Japan 1958
24 cm

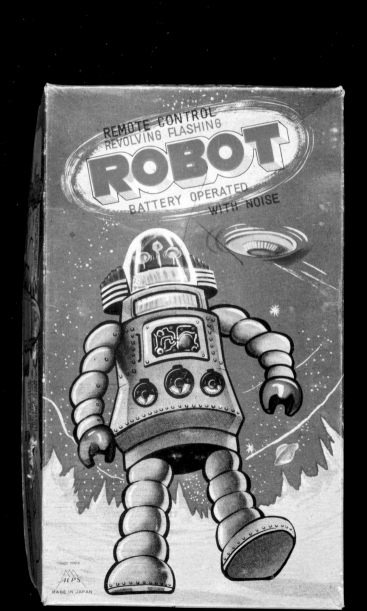

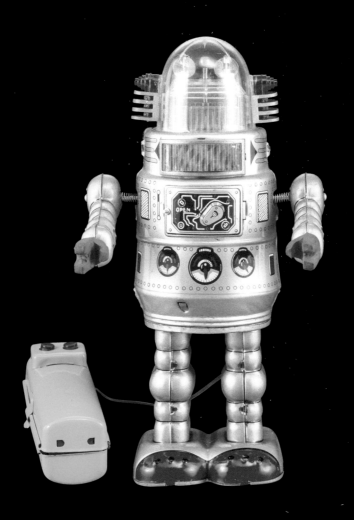

Robot
«Lantern Robot» /
«Powder Robot»
D: Linemar
battery operated
Japan 1958
19.7 cm

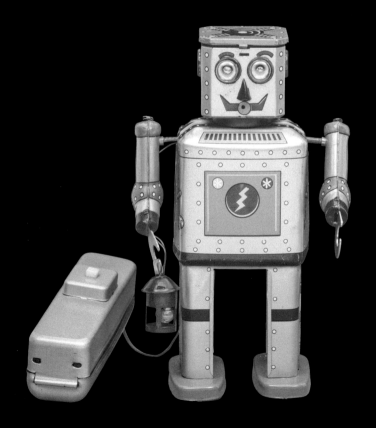

BATTERY OPERATED
REMOTE CONTROL

EARTH MAN

w/SOUNDING AND
BLINKING GUN

TRADE T.N MARK
JAPAN

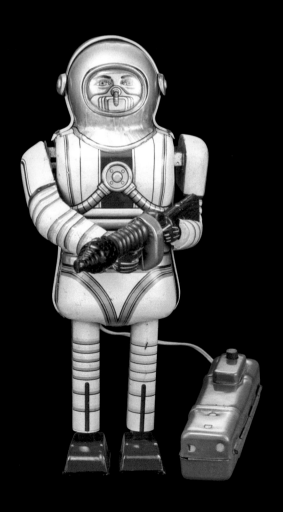

ROBOT ★★ CAR
WITH TUMBLING ROBOT

SPACE PATROL

IT'S
Cragston
for TOYS

10330

FRICTION TOY

TRADE MARK

ATC

MADE IN JAPAN

BATTERY OPERATED
REMOTE CONTROL
RoBoT

LINEMAR
BEST BY FAR

Spaceman Robot
P: Naito Shoten, AN
clockwork
Japan 1958
21 cm

MAGIC SPACE DOG

NON-STOP ACTION

TRADE MARK

KO

MADE IN JAPAN

BATTERY POWERED

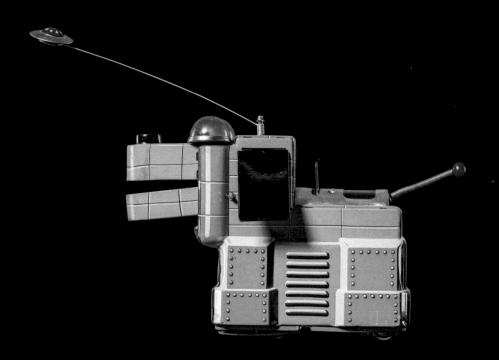

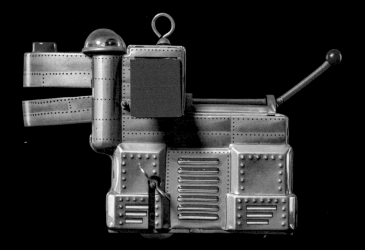

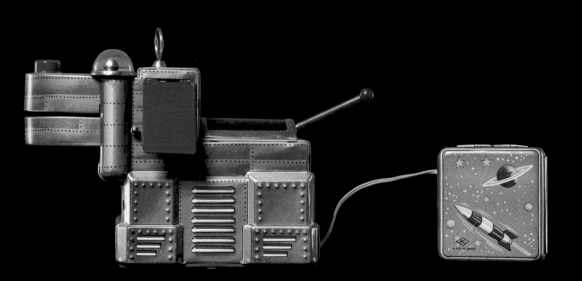

Robot Space Trooper
P: Yoshiya, KO
friction drive
Japan 1959
16.5 cm

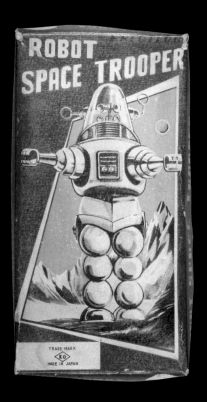

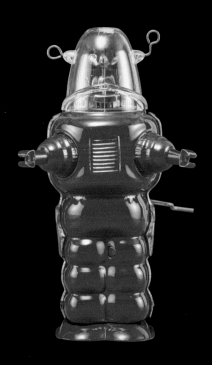

DUX-ASTROMAN

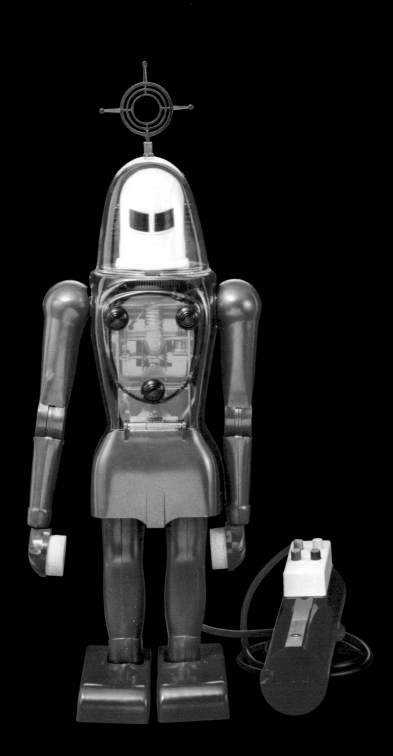

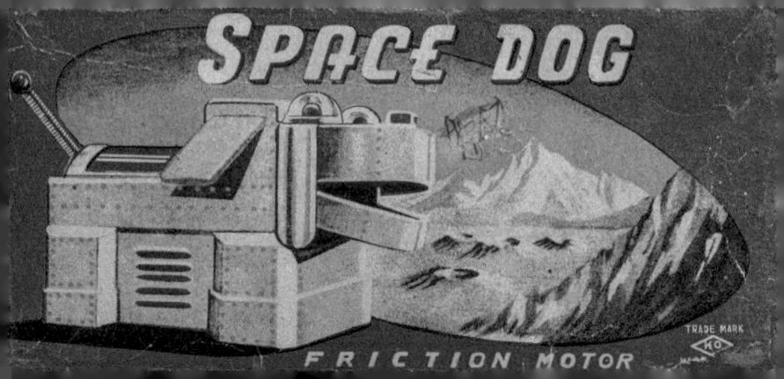
SPACE DOG
TRADE MARK
KO
FRICTION MOTOR

SP-1 Space Man Car
P: Usagiya
D: Linemar
friction
Japan late 1950's
7.5 cm

Road Construction Roller
P: Daiya
battery operated
Japan late 1950's
13 cm

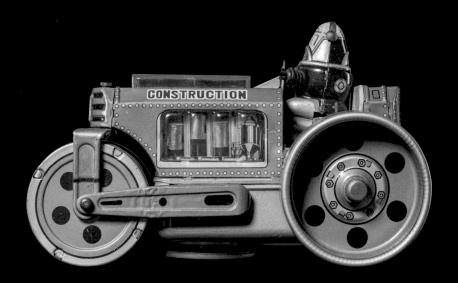

"NANDO"

il ROBOT a TELECOMANDO!

TELEVISION
ROBOT

MECHANICAL

BATTERY OPERATED
ROBOT

WHENEVER ROBOT HITS
OBSTACLE, HE TURNS HIS
FACE, BACKS AWAY AND
GOES FORTH IN
NEW DIRECTION

QUALITY TOY

MADE IN JAPAN

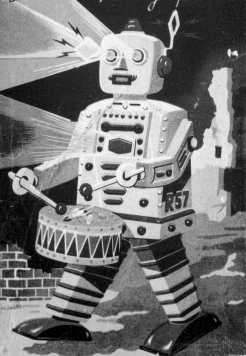

Remote Control

MUSICAL DRUMMER ROBOT

Battery Operated

R57

MADE T.N. MARK
JAPAN

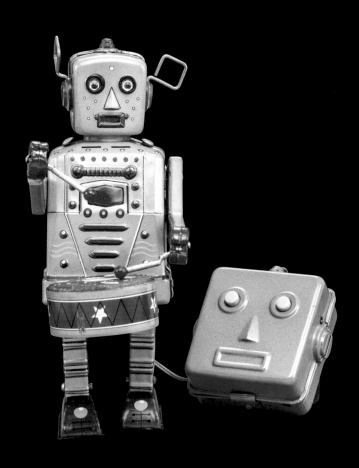

REMOTE CONTROL
BATTERY OPERATED
ROBOT
WITH PISTON ACTION

Made in JAPAN

SHOWA

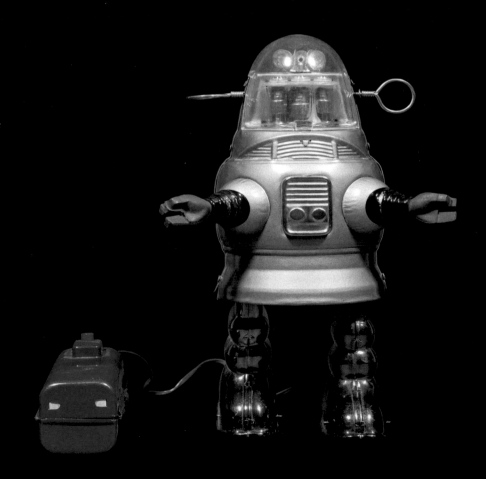

Inter Planet Space Captain
P: Naito Shoten, AN
D: A.C.E.
clockwork
Japan late 1950's
20 cm

Sparkling Mike
«Robot 5»
P: Sankei
clockwork
Japan late 1950's
19 cm

Space Man

BATTERY OPERATED
REMOTE CONTROL

SONSCO
JAPAN

ELECTRIC POWER
REMOTE CONTROL

SPACE
Robot
TROOPER

TRADE MARK
KO
MADE IN JAPAN

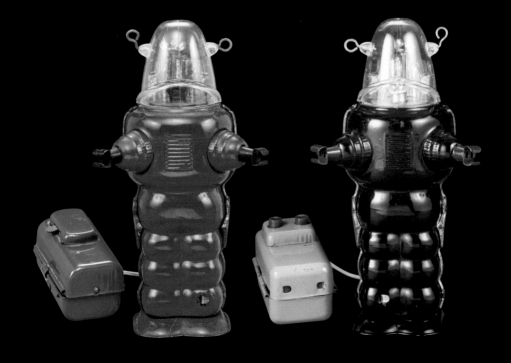

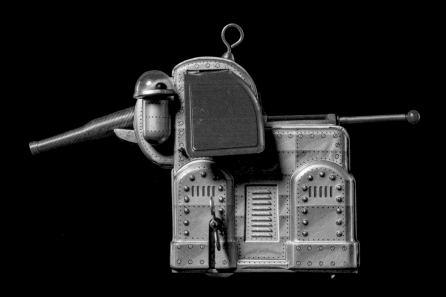

MECHANICAL

MoonRobot

TRADE 🌸 MARK

MADE IN JAPAN

PAT. PEND

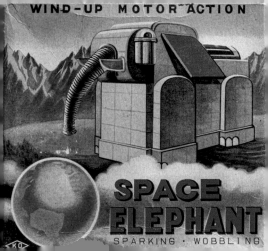

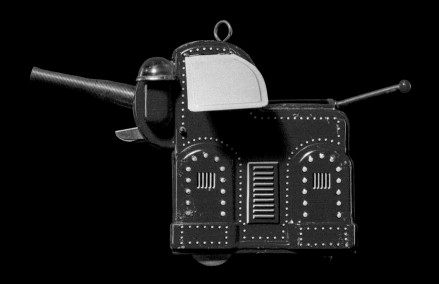

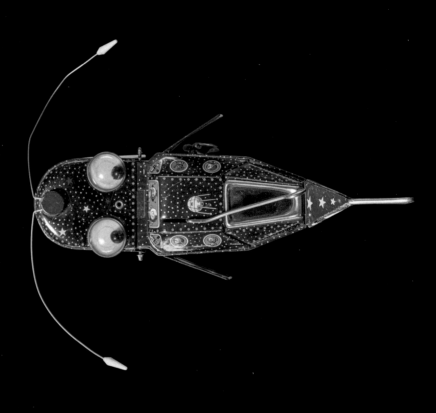

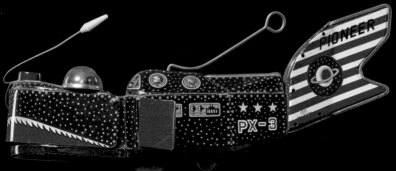

Smoking Robot
D: Linemar
battery operated
Japan 1960
30 cm

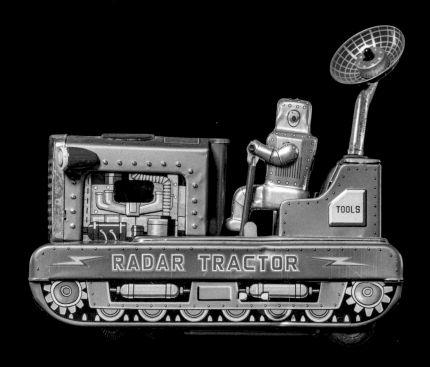

Non Stop Robot
«Lavender Robot»
P: Masudaya, MT
battery operated
Japan 1960
37.5 cm

Space Scout Robot

P: Yonezawa, Y
D: Frankonia
clockwork
Japan early 1960's
24 cm

MECHANICAL
CHIME TROOPER
ASTRONAUT

AS HE GOES
TONE OF
LOVELY CHIME

MADE IN JAPAN

ASC
REG TRADE MARK

Smoking Robot
P: Yonezawa, Y
battery operated
Japan early 1960's
30 cm

Moon Explorer
P: Yoshiya, KO
crank wound
Japan early 1960's
18 cm

RAPID FIRE
DUAL
BARRELS
SPACE TANK
SUPER ROBOT
TRADE S.H MARK
MADE IN JAPAN
FRICTION POWERED

MECHANICAL WALKING
SPACE
MAN
WITH MOVING ARMS
AND ANTENA

TRADE MARK
SY
JAPAN

MECHANICAL
THE
MEGO MAN

THE
MEGO
MAN

TRADE MARK
S·Y

BY MEGO

MADE IN JAPAN

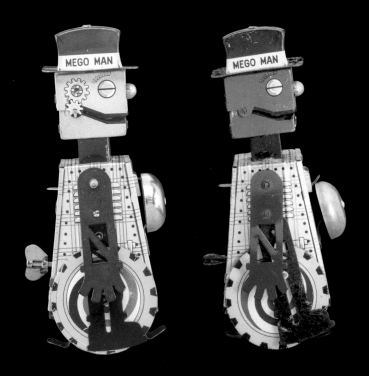

BATTERY OPERATED
TELEVISION
SPACEMAN

TRADE MARK
ALPS
MADE IN JAPAN

Cragstan
ASTRONAUT

AUTOMATIC   ACTIONS

X-70

-WALKS-
-STOPS-
-RAISES GUN-
-FIRES-
WITH
FLASHING
LIGHTS

-RATA TAT-
NOISE

-REVOLVING-
RADAR
ANTENNA

POWERED BY
BATTERY DRIVEN MOTOR
JAPAN

Cragstan

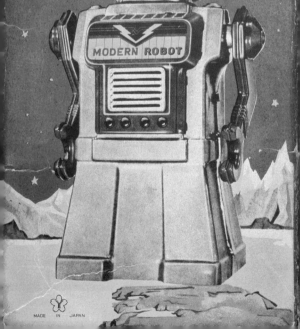

X-9 Space Robot Car
P: Masudaya
battery operated
Japan 1961
15 cm

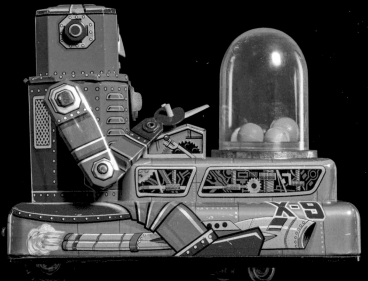

Giant Machine Man
P: Masudaya, MT
battery operated
Japan 1962
36.5 cm

Tremendous Mike
P: Aoshin, ASC
clockwork
Japan 1962
23 cm

38.5 cm

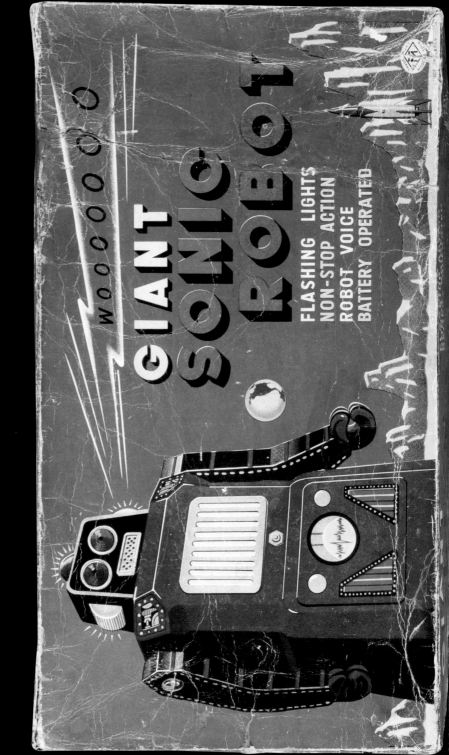

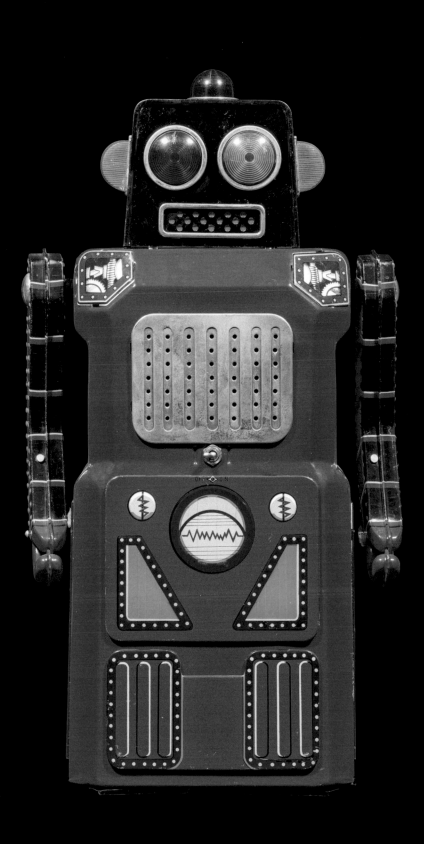

FRICTION POWERED

SPACE MAN

SPACE MAN

TRADE MARK

MADE IN JAPAN

BATTERY OPERATED
REMOTE CONTROL
PLANET ROBOT
KO
MADE IN JAPAN

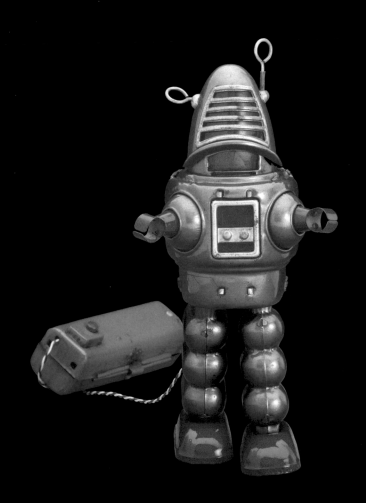

CHIEF ROBOTMAN

NEW ACTION TOY

HE
MOVES HEAD AROUND
SPINS RAD. R ANTENNAS

WALKS
STOPS
TURNS
ALL
AUTOMATIC

CHIEF ROBOTMAN

OPERATED BY
BATTERY POWERED MOTOR

MADE IN JAPAN

battery operated
Japan 1962
33 cm

STOP AND WALK

LIFT WALKIE-TALKIE

LISTEN TO SIGNALS
AND TALK BACK

FLASHING LIGHTS IN
HIS RECEIVING SET

BLUE LIGHT SIGNALS
IN HIS CLEAR PLASTIC
HELMET

WINKY! ROBOT

MECHANICAL

JUPITER ROBOT

BATTERY
OPERATED

SPACE
EXPLORER

JUPITER

SPACE EXPLORER

JUPITER

MADE IN JAPAN

ITEM NO. 801

SPACE
CONQUEROR

MAN OF TOMORROW

BATTERY
OPERATED
ACTION
STOP — GO
AND
POP-POP NOISE

US SPACE

TRADE DAIYA MARK
MADE IN JAPAN

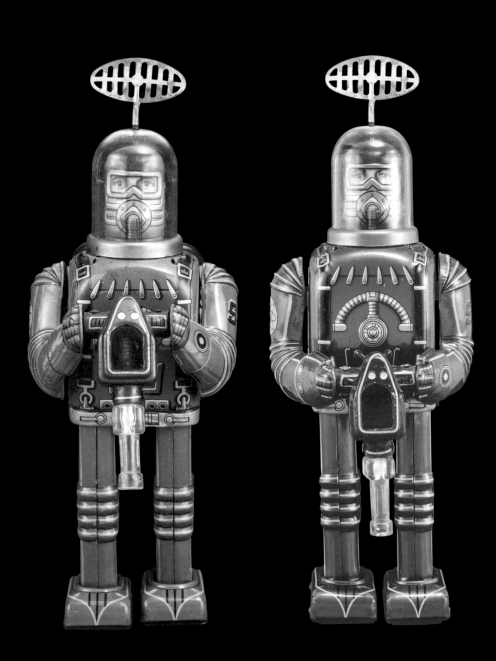

Diamond Planet Robot
P: Yonezawa, Y
clockwork
Japan 1962
26 cm

216

Diamond Planet Robot
P: Yonezawa, Y
clockwork
Japan 1962
26 cm

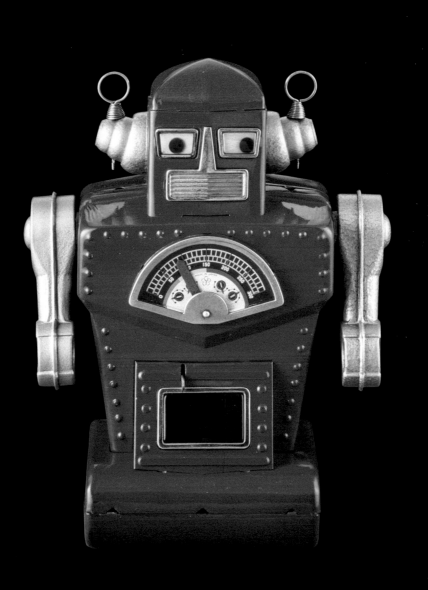

Walking Astronaut
MR. ROBOT

Space TOYS

by Asahi toy

® 618966
P. 230003
PP 48131

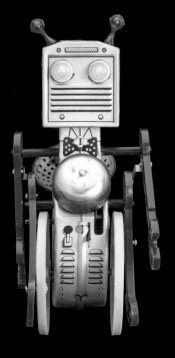

D: Cragstan
battery operated
Japan 1962
23.2 cm

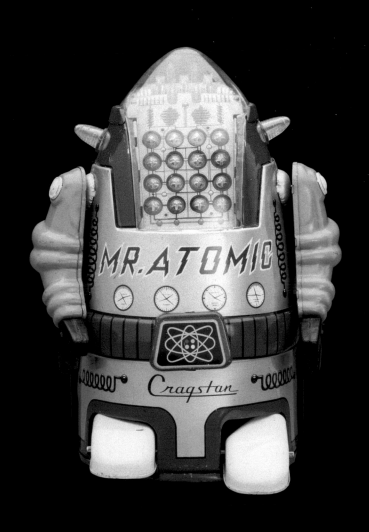

battery operated
Japan 1962
23.2 cm

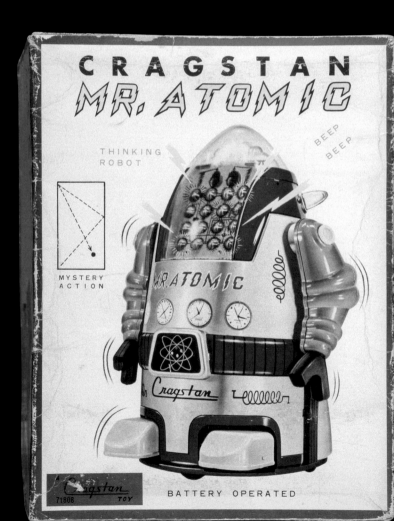

battery operated
Japan 1962
37.5 cm

Cragstan Astronaut .
P: Daiya
D: Cragstan
battery operated
Japan 1962
35.2 cm

Robot
«Hook Robot»
P: Waco
friction drive
Japan 1963
19 cm

Rosko Toy

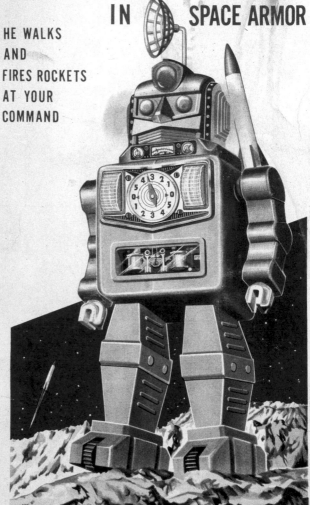

BATTERY OPERATED
REMOTE CONTROL

ROCKET MAN
IN SPACE ARMOR

HE WALKS
AND
FIRES ROCKETS
AT YOUR
COMMAND

ROSKO
R
TESTED

O88

TRADE MARK
ALPS
MADE IN JAPAN

ROSKO TOYS WITH IMAGINATION

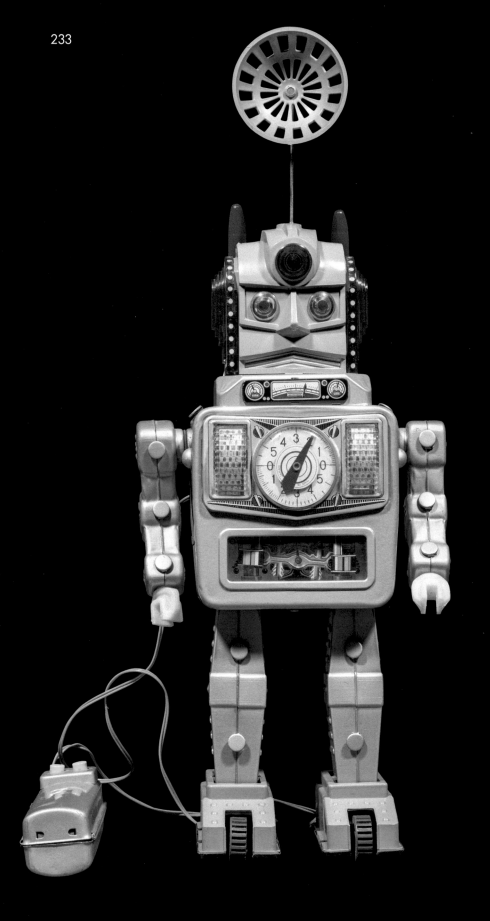

ADVANCED ROBOTMAN

CHIEF SMOKY

PUFFING STEAMLIKE SMOKE
LITED SEE THROUGH ACTION

CHIEF SMOKY

BATTERY POWERED
NON STOP

KO
MADE IN JAPAN

Space Explorer
P: Yonezawa, Y
clockwork
Japan 1963
24 cm

Robot Mighty 8
P: Masudaya, MT
battery operated
Japan 1963
29.8 cm

Mr. Mercury
P: Marx
battery operated
Japan 1963
33 cm

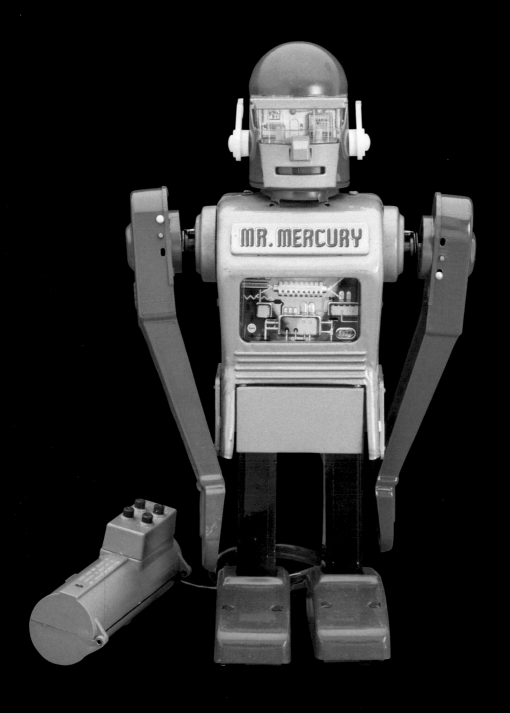

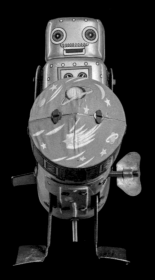

37.5 cm

P: Horikawa, SH
battery operated
Japan 1964
28 cm

Yonezawa, t
battery operated
Japan 1965
27.5 cm

TALKING ROBOT

BROADCASTS 4 DIFFERENT
MESSAGES
LOUD AND CLEAR

USE 1 "D" CELL BATTERY

U.K. PAT. P. NO 50386
PAT. APPLIED FOR IN U.S.A.

MADE IN JAPAN

BATTERY
POWERED
SOUND

ON OFF
SWITCH

FRICTION
POWERED
ROBOT

ITEM No. 2525

ITEM No. 2525

ROBBY ROBOT
WITH SPARKING ACTION

ITEM. No. **809**

MADE IN JAPAN

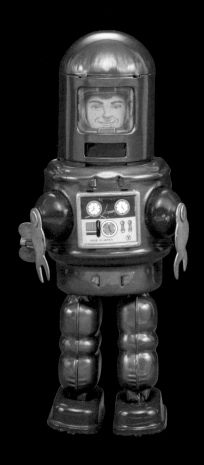

BATTERY OPERATED
MIGHTY ROBOT

MYSTERY ACTION
TRANSPARENT MACHINE AND LIGHT UP ACTION

MADE IN JAPAN

BATTERY OPERATED
REMOTE CONTROL

HIGH - WHEEL
ROBOT

KO

MADE IN JAP

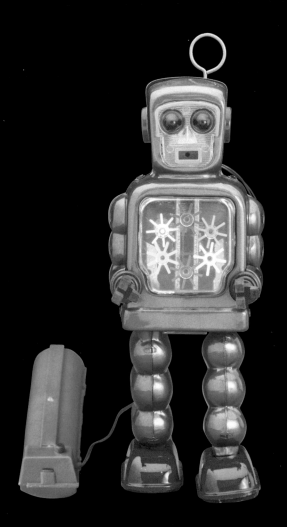

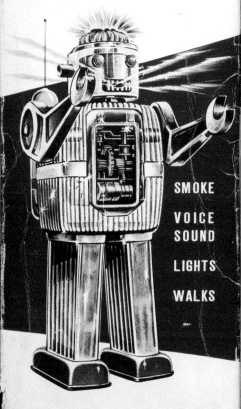

RANGER ROBOT

SMOKE

VOICE
SOUND

LIGHTS

WALKS

MOVING ARMS
BATTERY POWERED

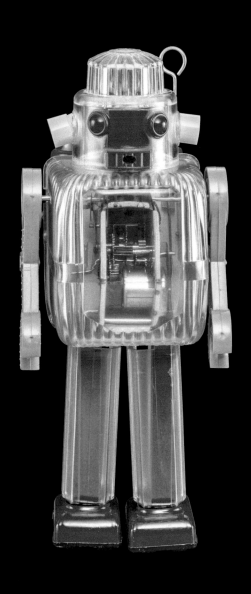

Commander Robot
«Orange Robot» / «R-Robot»
P: Yonezawa, Y
clockwork
Japan mid 1960's
26.5 cm

FRICTION POWERED
X-27 EXPLORER

Y TRADE MARK

MADE IN JAPAN

ITEM NO. 805

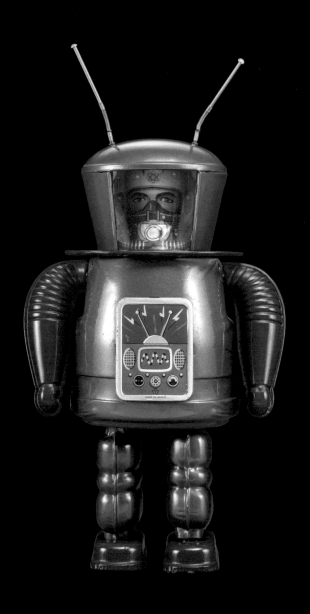

WIND-UP
FRICTION POWERED
ASTRO-SCOUT

3

MADE IN JAPAN   3192   A FRANKONIA TOY

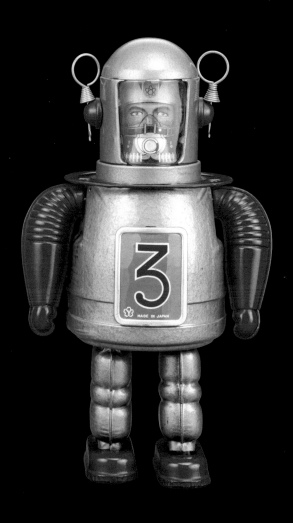

BATTERY OPERATED
SUPER RADAR TRACTOR

MYSTERY ACTION
REVOLVING ENGINE
REVOLVING RADAR
ANTENNA

T-27 SUPER RADAR TRACTOR

A FRANKON'A TOY

MADE IN JAPAN

MECHANICAL

SWINGING
BABY
ROBOT

BATTERY OPERATED
MOON
EXPLORER

TRADE MARK
ALPS
MADE IN JAPAN

clockwork
Japan 1966
14.3 cm

BATTERY OPERATED
SILVER RAY
SECRET WEAPON
SPACE SCOUT

BIG FEATURES:
* REALISTIC STRIDE * FLASHING CAMERA
* POP-OUT CHEST * BIG MACHINE GUN
* GO-STOP ACTION SOUND AND BLINK

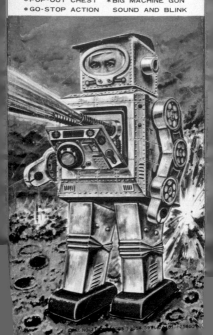

Astronaut
P: Daiya
battery operated
Japan 1966
35.2 cm

Hi-Bouncer Moon Scout
P: Marx
battery operated
Japan 1967
29.5 cm

280

Space Robot
«Conehead Robot»
P: Yonezawa, Y
clockwork
Japan 1967
22 cm

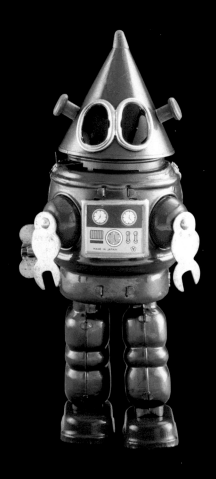

MECHANICAL
TELEVISION
SPACEMAN

TRADE MARK
ALPS
MADE IN JAPAN

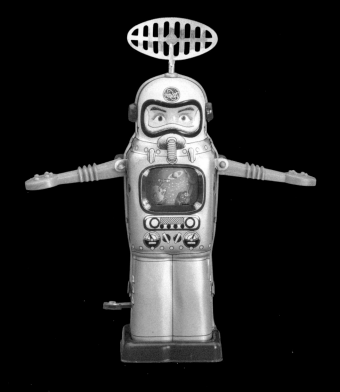

Missile Robot
P: Alps
battery operated
Japan 1967
44 cm

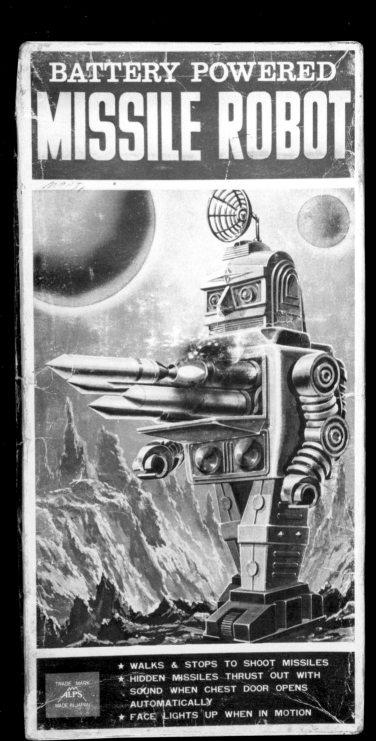

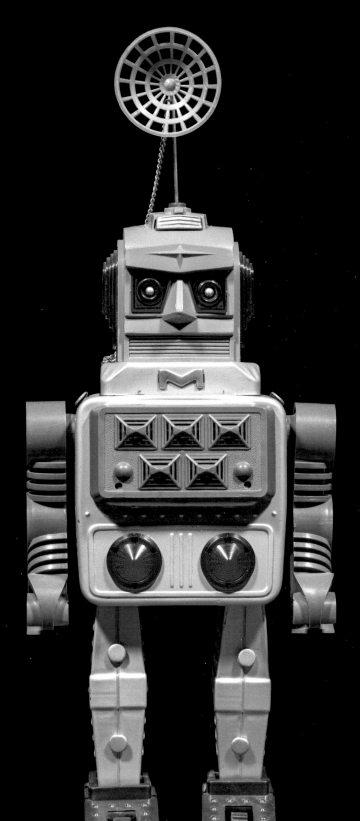

BATTERY OPERATED
SPACE
EXPLORER

ITEM NO. 802 MADE IN JAPAN

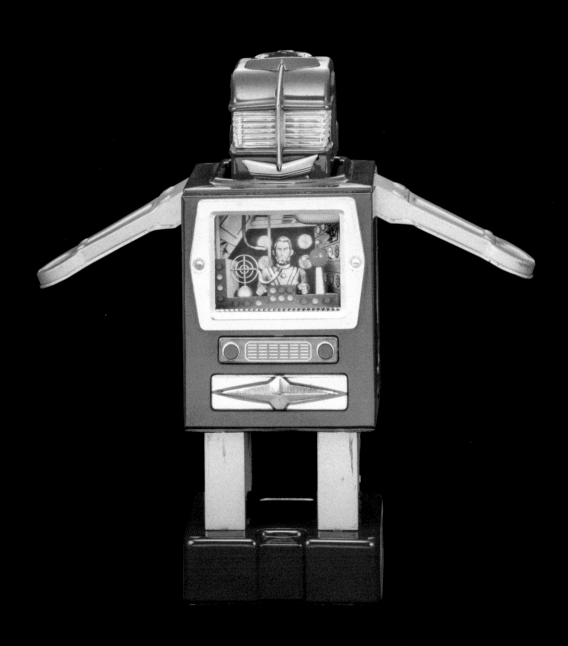

HIGH-WHEEL ROBOT
WIND-UP MOTOR

- TRANSPARENT MACHINE ACTION
- SPARKLING ACTION
- TELESCOPIC AERIAL
- ATTACHED KEY
- WALKING ACTION

日本製

JTA
ST
SAFETY TOY
T1029008

K.O.
MADE IN JAPAN

AERIAL

NOTICE

WIND-UP MOTOR **HIGH-WHEEL ROBOT**

Colonel Hap Hazard
P: Marx
battery operated
Japan 1967
29.5

MECHANICAL
MIGHTY ROBOT

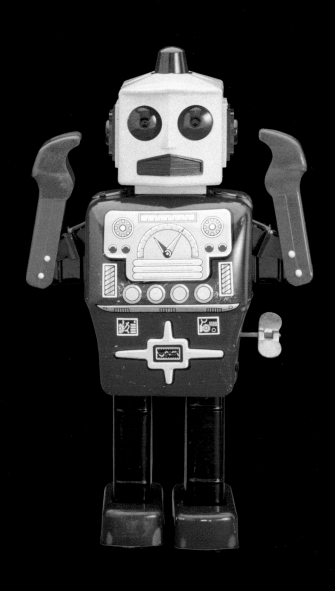

MECHANICAL WIND-UP
ATOMIC ROBOT

★ WALKING FORWARD.
★ TURNING HEAD
  AND HANDS.
★ WITH NOISE.

ITEM No. 819

MADE IN JAPAN

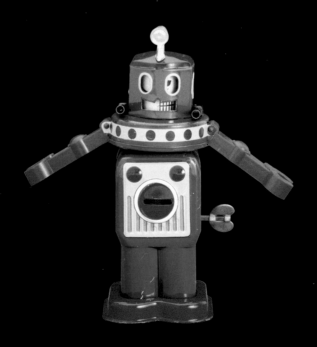

BATTERY POWERED

ROBOTANK-Z

SPACE ROBOT

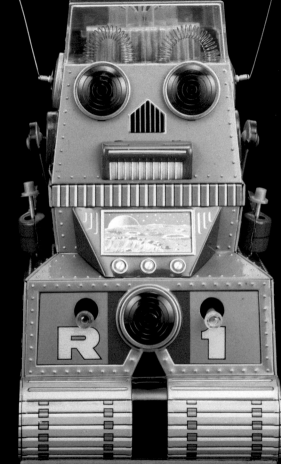

BATTERY OPERATED

MARS KING

WITH T.V. AND SIREN

CATERPILLAR

TRADE S.H MARK

MADE IN JAPAN

テレホン ロボット

PAT. P

ITEM NO. 800

4347

TRADE MARK
Y
IN JAPAN

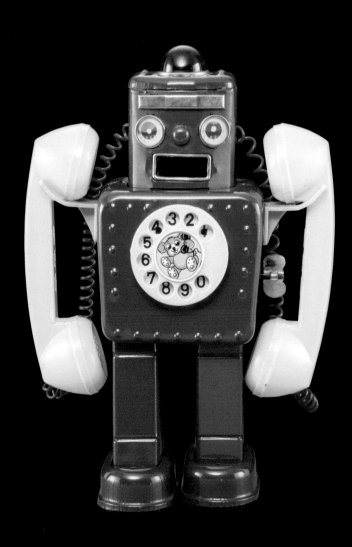

THUNDER ROBOT

BATTERY OPERATED

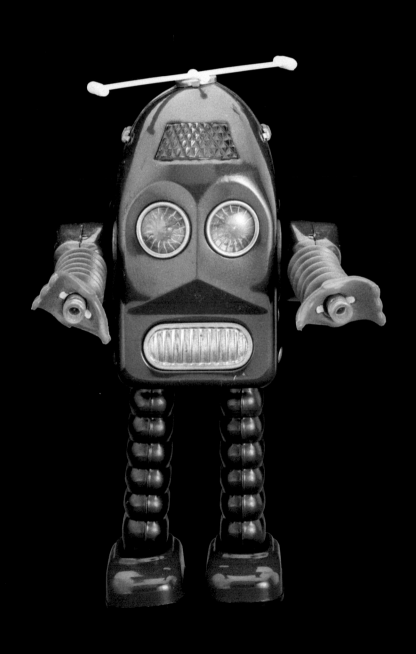

battery operated
Japan 1968
28 cm

BATTERY OPERATED
MR. PATROL
WITH SIREN

BATTERY OPERATED

Blink-A-Gear ROBOT

★ WALKS WITH SWINGING ARMS
★ GEARS WITH MACHINE NOISE
★ COLORED GEARS WITH
   BLINKING LIGHT
★ BIG EYES BLINK

PATENT. P25391

R - 81

MADE IN JAPAN

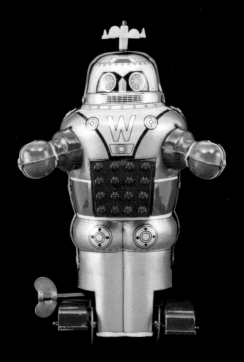

Mechanical Walking Robot
P: Noguchi, N
clockwork
Japan late 1960's
10 cm

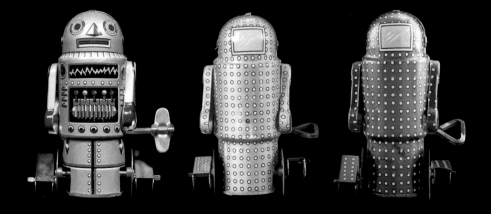

MARS
EXPLORER

MARS EXPLORER
EXPLORING, HE RUNS IN THE SPACE.
HE SUDDENLY STOPS RUNNING.
HIS MASK AND DOOR OPEN, AND TWO GUNS POP OUT
OF CHEST FIRING AND BLINKING WITH REALISTIC SOUND.
GUN RETRACT, MASK AND DOOR CLOSE.
CONTINUE RUNNING AGAIN.

BATTERY OPERATED
PAT. NO. 41941, 41942, 18743, 13948

MADE IN JAPAN

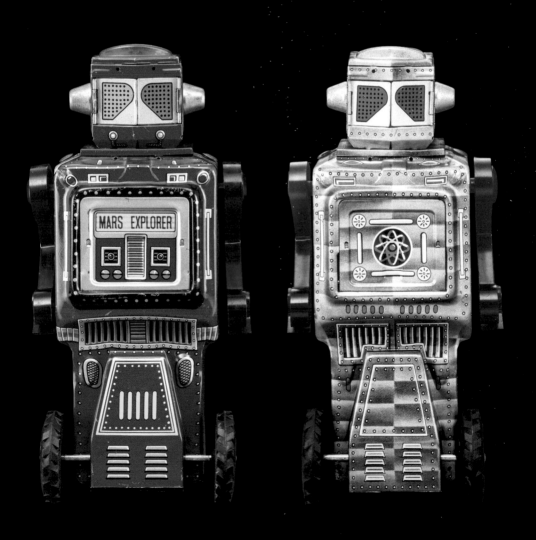

WIND-UP
LUNAR ROBOT

WIND-UP LUNAR ROBOT

3235

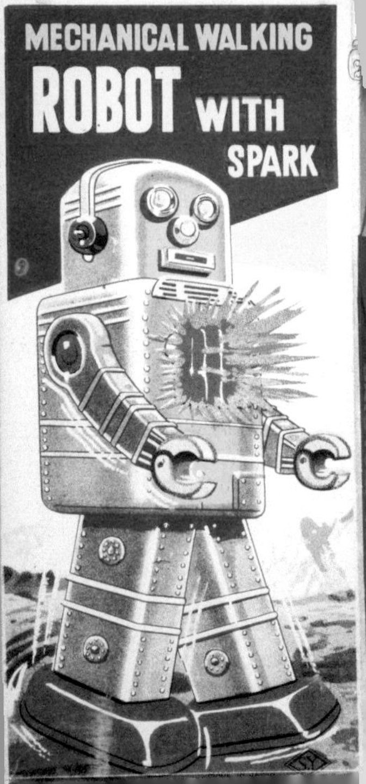

MECHANICAL WALKING
ROBOT WITH
SPARK

BATTERY OPERATED
SPACE
COMMANDER

AUTOMATIC ACTIONS
BUMP'N GO
SWING OPEN DOOR
BLINKING & SHOOTING GUNS
REALISTIC FIRING NOISE

PATENT No. 3971·19054   TRADE **S.H** MARK

MADE IN JAPAN

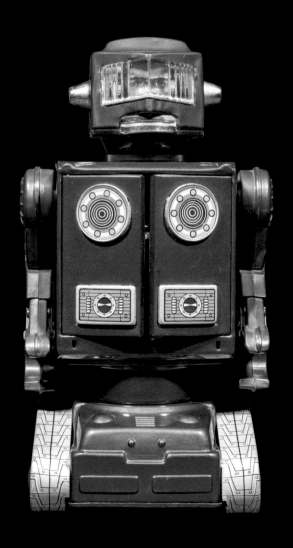

Astroman
P: Nomura, TN
clockwork
Japan late 1960's
23.5 cm

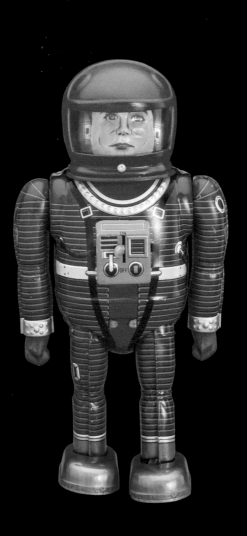

SPACE ROBOT

WITH **T.V. CAMERA** AND **SCREEN**

BATTERY OPERATED

ACTION
PLANET ROBOT
KEY WOUND MOTOR
SPARKY

日本製

KO
JAPAN

JTA
ST
SAFETY TOY
T1029007

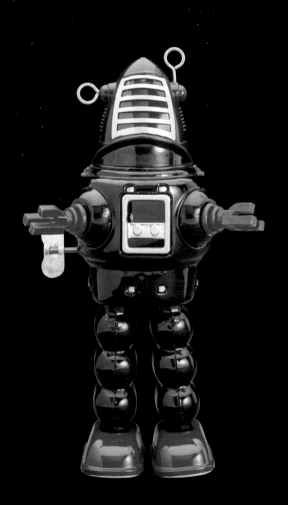

ЕЛОЧНОЙ
ИЛЛЮМИНАЦИИ

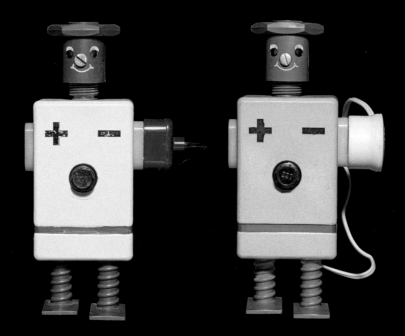

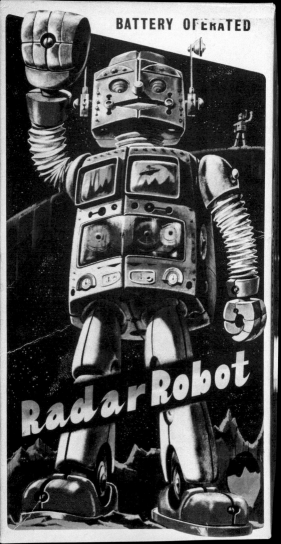

Busy Cart Robot
P: Horikawa, SH
battery operated
Japan 1972
29 cm

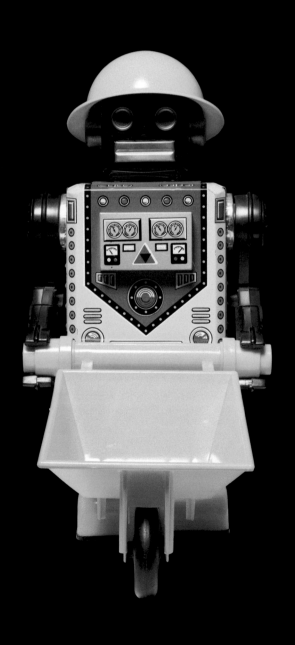

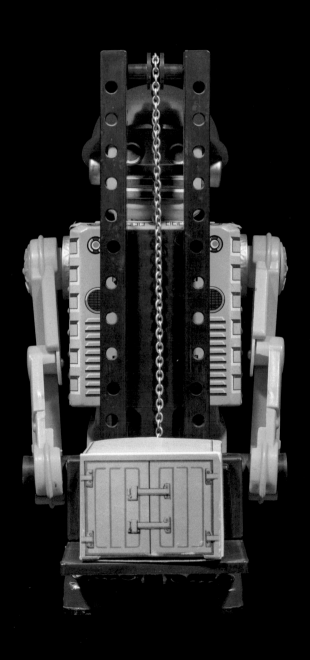

Robot
P: Iskra Plant - Taganrog
clockwork
Russia mid 1970's
18 cm

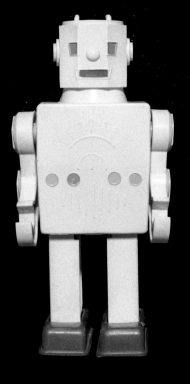

PES PLUTO

MADE IN CZECHOSLOVAKIA

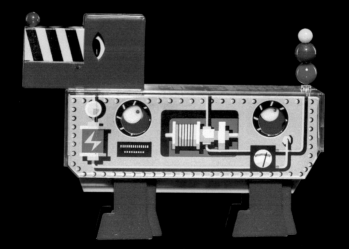

« Toys are really not as innocent as they look. Toys and games are the preludes to serious ideas. »[2]

Charles Eames

[2] Eames Demetrios and Carla Hartman, eds, *Essential Eames: Words & Pictures* (Weil am Rhein: Vitra Design Museum, 2017), 144.

Colophon

Editors: Rolf Fehlbaum, Fifo Stricker
Consulting experts: Dirk Gadomski, Gernot Münk
Editing: Barbara Hauß
Photos and Films: Luka Dogan, André Giese, Moritz Herzog

Design: Thorsten Romanus
Distribution: Pinar Yildiz
Printing: DZA Druckerei zu Altenburg GmbH
Paper: Gardamatt Art, 170 g/qm
Typeface: VFutura

First published by the Vitra Design Museum

Vitra Design Museum
Charles-Eames-Str. 2
79576 Weil am Rhein
Germany
verlag@design-museum.de
www.design-museum.de

Printed and bound in Germany
© Vitra Design Museum 2022

All rights reserved. No part of this publication may be reproduced,
stored in a retrieval system or transmitted in any form or by
any means, electronic, mechanical, photo-copying, recording
or otherwise, without written prior consent of the publisher.
The German National Library has listed this publication in the
German National Bibliography; detailed bibliographical data
is available at http://dnb.dnb.de

ISBN 978-3-945852-54-5